THE 6-WEEK CHALLENGE BLOOD SUGAR DIET

TAKE CONTROL OF YOUR HEALTH AND LOSE WEIGHT FAST

ZOBLIT

Original ISBN 13: 978-1-911147-28-2

ISBN - 978-1-911147-28-2 - 978-1-911147-29-9 - 978-1-911147-30-5 (Paperback)

Zoblit ltd

Unit A Vulcan House, Vulcan Road, Leicester, LE5 3EB

A catalogue record of this book is available from the British Library

New Paperback Cover Design by Manoj Patil (The Rubixion)

Slim Nourish Glow Cover design © 2016 Manoj Patil - The Rubixion

Edited by Nextquisite Ltd, London

Printed in the United Kingdom

Disclaimer

Please note some recipes may contain nuts or traces of nuts. Nut allergy sufferers should avoid such recipes.

The Information and advice contained in this book are intended as a general guide and may contain typographical and or content errors. The author and the publisher do not offer any legal or other professional advice. Where required always consult with the appropriate professional or qualified practitioner. Any application of the ideas and information within this book is at the reader's sole discretion and risk. The Publisher hereby exclude all liability to the extent permitted by law for any errors or omissions in this book and for any loss, damage or expense (whether direct or indirect) suffered by a third party relying on any information contained in this book.

BREAKFAST & BRUNCH

APPETIZERS & SNACKS

LIGHT LUNCHES

DINNERS

DESSERTS

INTRODUCTION

WHAT IS THE BLOOD SUGAR DIET? IS IT FOR ME?

DIABETES IS A GLOBAL EPIDEMIC. DON'T BE THE NEXT VICTIM

What exactly is the blood sugar diet and why should you be sitting up and taking notice? There are so many diets, and with new ones coming along every day you might think that this is just another faddy idea that will pass with the season. This is not the case, so please, take the time to read this short introduction.

The blood sugar diet is a simple approach to healthy eating developed by scientists to fight back against the tidal wave of obesity and adult-onset diabetes that threatens to engulf much of the world today. It is based on eating delicious natural foods that are easily prepared at home. It works quickly, bringing substantial weight loss in just a few weeks and it also normalises blood sugar, reducing the risk of developing type 2 diabetes and in many cases even reversing diabetes after it has been diagnosed.

In the past, before modern Western diets and lifestyles became prevalent, diabetes was relatively rare. The disease is now becoming more and more common. According to the World Health Organization (WHO), in 1980 there were 108 million people around the world with diabetes; by 2014 that figure had shot up to 422 million.

There are two types of diabetes: Type 1, which usually starts in childhood, occurs when the pancreas does not produce enough insulin, and it requires daily administration of insulin. Type 1 diabetes is still relatively uncommon and it is not known what causes it. Type 2 diabetes, which is almost always diagnosed in adults, results from the body's ineffective use of insulin. The vast majority of people with diabetes today have this second type and it is mainly caused by an unhealthy diet, being overweight and not getting enough exercise.

ONE PERSON IN 16 IN THE UK HAS DIABETES

REDUCE YOUR RISK OF DEVELOPING TYPE 2 DIABETES

Diabetes causes a range of symptoms, including excessive thirst and hunger, needing to urinate often, weight loss, changes in vision and extreme tiredness. It is also deadly. People with diabetes are two to three times more likely to have a heart attack or stroke. Diabetes leads to blindness, kidney failure and lower limb amputation. In 2012, more than 3.6 million people died of diabetes and complications arising from high blood sugar. WHO predicts that diabetes will be the seventh leading cause of death by 2030.

This is not an epidemic that's taking place in far-off places, it's happening right here, in our own country. By early 2016, more than 3.5 million people in the UK had been diagnosed with diabetes. Many more are living with the symptoms, without knowing what is wrong with them. According to the NHS, the number of people with diabetes in the UK has trebled since 1996 and will reach 5 million by 2025.

The thing about type 2 diabetes is that it is largely preventable. You can lower your risk considerably by controlling your blood sugar levels, maintaining a healthy weight and exercising regularly. Even if type 2 diabetes has already been diagnosed, you can manage, and in some cases even reverse it, by improving your diet and increasing your physical activity levels. Our diet plan is an important step in getting you back on track.

In this book you will find 78 delicious recipes, all of which have been carefully developed to help you reach your target blood sugar levels and weight. If you have not already done so, you should have a simple blood test done to measure your blood sugar levels. The test should be carried out while you are fasting, which means you should not eat or drink anything except water for at least 8 hours before the blood test. Opinions vary slightly on what constitutes normal or optimal blood sugar levels. According to Diabetes.co.uk, these should be:

Normal: 3.9 to 5.5 mmol/l (70 to 100 mg/dl)
Prediabetes: 5.6 to 7.0 mmol/l (101 to 126 mg/dl)
Diabetes: above 7.0 mmol/l (126 mg/dl)

If your results are in the prediabetes or diabetes range your doctor will want to discuss these with you and will probably suggest changes to your diet and lifestyle and may even want you to begin taking medication. It is always best to consult with your doctor or a qualified health care provider before making any radical changes to your diet, including the ones we suggest in this book. If you have some health problems, or are taking certain medications, a very low-calorie diet may not be ideal for you. Discuss it with your doctor first.

You should also weigh yourself before you begin to check whether your Body Mass Index (BMI) is within the normal ranges of 18 to 25. The best way to check if your BMI is to use one of the many online calculators.

If your blood sugar levels are raised or your BMI is above the desirable range, you will want to start with an intensive induction phase of up to six weeks during which you eat no more than 800 calories each day. If this proves too severe, you may want to start at 1000 or 1200 calories a day.

The calorie intake of a “normal” adult is usually calculated at about 2,000 per day. That number is very generic because it doesn’t take into account weight, age, gender or levels of activity. However, if you cut your intake to between 800 and 1200 calories a day, you will lose weight and quite rapidly. How rapidly will depend on your current weight and how much exercise you get.

You may have heard that a very low calorie intake is unhealthy. The latest scientific research does not agree, although it is essential that you eat healthy food, like the recipes included in this book.

The recipes have been divided into five chapters for meals and snacks throughout the day so that you can shop and plan ahead. Each recipe tells you how many people it will serve and how many calories there are in each serving. Most of our recipes are for two to four servings. If you are preparing them for yourself you can half them and refrigerate what you don't eat for the next day. Use the calorie count for each recipe to put together your daily menus at the desired calorie intake.

You will begin to lose weight within a few days and your blood sugar levels will also begin to drop quite quickly. As you reach your goals you can begin to add more calories.

THE SIX-WEEK PLAN THAT WILL CHANGE YOUR LIFE

You have seen in the introduction that adopting the blood sugar diet can help normalise your blood sugar levels and bring you back to a healthy weight. But it is not just by adopting this diet that you will achieve total wellness. We suggest that you take six weeks to begin a complete overhaul of your diet, exercise and lifestyle choices. We have identified six general wellness areas and we suggest that you focus on one of them each week to restore and improve your health. The areas are healthy eating, staying active, sleeping well, stress management, being connected, and finding direction and passion in your life.

WEEK ONE FOCUS: HEALTHY EATING

We'd like you to start the plan to change your life by really thinking about what you eat and how it affects your health. Even before you start the diet, you might like to try keeping a food journal to see exactly what you eat and when you eat it. You should also go through your kitchen cupboards and throw out foods that are laden with unhealthy refined flour, sugar and additives.

If you are following the diet plan recommended in the body of this book, you will be well on your way to achieving wellness already. But more generally speaking, there are a few basic rules to consider when planning a healthy diet for yourself and your family, irrespective of specific health issues:

- Eat real foods: Vegetables, fruits, whole grains, nuts, cheese, butter, olive oil, fish and meat are all foods that your grandparents would recognise and eat. These are real foods.
- Prepare these real foods yourself: You don't need to be told that readymade supermarket meals and the like will be full of unhealthy additives, such as sugar,

trans-fats, preservatives and artificial colourings and flavourings. If you buy fresh real foods and prepare them at home you know exactly what you are eating.

- Eat real foods as close to their natural state as possible: This doesn't necessarily mean they should be eaten raw, but enjoy them cooked simply so that their natural flavours can shine through. Some of the world's best-loved cuisines, such as Italian and Greek, are quite austere and based on high-quality ingredients that are cooked and served as close to nature as possible.
- Eat foods that are locally grown and in season: Foods that have been harvested before they are mature, kept in cool stores then shipped halfway round the world are unlikely to be full of the nutrients you need for optimum health.
- Eat joyfully: Devote time to the preparation of food and take time to enjoy it, preferably in the company of friends and family. Even if you are eating alone, don't gobble it down on the run or while watching TV.

WEEK TWO FOCUS: STAYING ACTIVE

This week we'd like you to maintain your healthy eating plan, but also to take time to think about your exercise goals. Regular physical activity brings so many benefits it's difficult to know where to start. Perhaps most importantly, exercise can help manage health conditions and combat disease. It can prevent and control heart disease, stroke, type 2 diabetes, high blood pressure, cholesterol levels, osteoporosis, arthritis and many types of cancer, to name a few.

Exercise can also stop you gaining weight or help maintain weight loss. When you engage in physical activity, you burn calories. The more intense the activity, the more calories you burn. If you don't have time to work out, get more active throughout the day in simple ways, for example, by walking to work or taking the stairs instead of the lift.

Exercise boosts your mood and increases your energy levels. As you exercise more, you will look and feel so much better, which will encourage you to engage in more exercise. It's a virtuous circle. Exercise will also help you to sleep better and to enjoy a more rewarding sex life.

As you can see, starting a fitness programme may be one of the best things you can do for your health. Remember that you don't have to run a marathon, or even join a gym if you don't want to. In fact, when you're designing your personal fitness programme, think carefully about what you like doing and have time for.

Try to make exercise a fun part of your daily routine; that way you are more likely to stick with it. There's no point signing up for an expensive pilates course across town if your work or family commitments will make it difficult to go. If you have a high pressure job, do you really want another fixed "appointment" locked into your already packed schedule? For you, making a date to power walk with a friend once a week, playing tennis with family or friends on the weekends, and some basic yoga or stretching 2–3 days a week at home, might be enough. And think about booking that ski holiday or walking tour as this will encourage you to get in shape before you leave.

WEEK THREE FOCUS: SLEEPING WELL

By week three you will begin to notice that your trousers or skirts are looser at the waist and the scales should also show that you have lost a few pounds. The benefits of your healthy eating and exercise plans will be kicking in so keep them up as you head into the third week of your new life. Now is the time to think about how well you sleep. Resting plays a vital role in maintaining good health and getting enough quality sleep will help protect your mental and physical health, as well as improve your quality of life. Sleep helps your brain to work efficiently. While you are sleeping, your brain is preparing for the next day, forming new pathways to help you learn and remember information.

Sleep allows your mind and body to restore themselves. For example, sleep is involved in healing and repair of your heart and blood vessels and ongoing sleep deficiency is linked to an increased risk of heart disease, stroke, high blood pressure, kidney disease and diabetes. Sleep deficiency has also been linked to depression, suicide and an increased risk of dementia.

There are a number of things you can do to improve the quality of your sleep:

- Establish a sleep routine by going to bed and waking up at the same time each day: This will regulate your body clock, making it easier to fall asleep and stay asleep all night.
- Daily exercise: Vigorous exercise is best, but even light exercise helps. Exercise at any time of day, but not in the 2–3 hours before you go to bed.
- Evaluate your room and bed: Your bedroom should be cool and free from noise and light. Your bed should comfortable and supportive. Have comfortable pillows and make the room attractive and inviting for sleep.
- Avoid alcohol, cigarettes and heavy meals in the evening as these can disrupt sleep.
- Wind down and relax for an hour or two before bedtime: Your body needs time to shift into sleep mode, so spend time doing a calming activity such as reading. Using an electronic device such as a laptop can make it hard to fall asleep, because the particular type of light emanating from the screens of these devices is activating to the brain.

WEEK FOUR: STRESS MANAGEMENT

This week, in addition to maintaining your healthy eating plan, exercise programme, and sleeping well focus, we'd like you zero in on managing stress and living serenely. When stressed, the body thinks it is under attack and switches to "fight or flight" mode, releasing a mixture of hormones and chemicals such as cortisol and adrenaline to prepare the body for physical action. This causes a series of reactions, from blood being diverted to muscles to shutting down unnecessary bodily functions such as digestion. Stress is not always a bad thing. Sometimes it can help you focus and react appropriately, but long term stress can cause considerable damage, both physically and mentally.

Stress management is about taking charge of your life and the way you deal with problems. No matter how stressful your life seems, there are steps you can take to relieve the pressure and regain control. Try these solutions:

- Learn to say no and avoid situations and people that stress you out.
- Learn to express your feelings instead of bottling them up inside.
- Be solution-oriented: Think "how can I solve this problem", and go ahead.
- Be willing to compromise.
- Think positive and look at the big picture.

- Keep a sense of proportion and your sense of humour.
- Be willing to forgive.
- Follow a healthy diet, get plenty of sleep and exercise regularly. These are all great ways to reduce stress.

WEEK FIVE FOCUS: BEING CONNECTED

By week five many of you will be close to reaching your weight and overall health goals. This will bring a feeling of satisfaction and the desire to move forward with your life. This week, we'd like you to stay focused on healthy eating, staying active, sleeping well and stress management, and also to take the time to think about how you interact with the world. We all need to feel connected, firstly to ourselves and then to the world around us. Feelings of loneliness and isolation can be devastating to your health and often lead to unhealthy lifestyle choices such as overeating, binge drinking and even addiction, whether it be to drugs, alcohol, sex, gambling or even work.

There are many ways to re-connect with yourself, with others and with nature.

- Meditation: Sign up for a course in mindful meditation and learn how to really feel your emotions and accept them. Get back in touch with you innermost self.
- Switch off: Ironically, this may be one of the best ways to connect. Set aside an hour, a day or a weekend and deliberately disconnect from your everyday life. Switch off your cell phone, don't compulsively check your texts or email or even watch TV. Be silent. Spend time in peaceful harmony with yourself.
- Be kind to yourself and others. Donate some of your time or money to those less fortunate than yourself. Acts of kindness can be as simple as smiling or greeting strangers or being courteous in everyday situations.
- Find time to connect with nature.

WEEK SIX FOCUS: FINDING DIRECTION & PASSION IN LIFE

Congratulations! You have reached the last week of your makeover plan. By now you should be feeling and looking your best. During this final week we would like you to stick with your healthy eating plan, exercise routine, sleeping well focus, stress

FIND PASSION IN YOUR LIFE

management and staying connected, but we would also like you to look at your long term goals. You only have this one life, so make the most of it. Take time to ask yourself if you are truly happy in the choices you have made and remember that you can always make changes to your life story. If you feel that your life lacks purpose or meaning, if you are constantly tired and discouraged or challenged by anxiety and feelings of inadequacy, you will not be enjoying good health or total wellness. Take the time to examine your life. Try to explain it to yourself as though you were talking about someone else. Step back and try to get some perspective on it, then decide what you can do to improve things.

Once you have decided on the people, job, places and experiences that are important to you, pursue them all with passion. Is your job all wrong for you? Maybe you would prefer to set up your own small business and experience the satisfaction of being your own boss. Perhaps it is time to retire and dedicate yourself to the things that truly interest you. There are many choices to be made in life. Don't take anything for granted.

BREAKFAST & BRUNCH

Some people love breakfast. They get up early and potter about in the kitchen, making tasty food to share. If that's your thing, there's plenty in this chapter for you. But if you don't like to eat breakfast, don't! Wait until you feel like eating. Just make sure you have something healthy to hand when hunger strikes. A small pottle of yoghurt or a handful of fresh berries or nuts are ideal.

BLUEBERRY & SPINACH SMOOTHIES

SERVES: 2

Ingredients

300 g (2 cups) fresh blueberries
50 g (1 cup) fresh spinach leaves
250 ml (1 cup) plain yoghurt
120 ml (½ cup) unsweetened almond milk

Special Tip: *You can whizz up this smoothie in just a few seconds. It's ideal for busy weekday mornings. Choose non-fat, low-fat or full-fat yoghurt, as preferred.*

Method:

170 CALORIES

Place two tall glasses in the freezer to chill while you prepare the smoothies. Reserve a few whole blueberries to garnish.

Combine the remaining blueberries, spinach, yoghurt and almond milk in a blender and blend until smooth.

Pour into the glasses, sprinkle the reserved blueberries on top, and serve.

AVOCADO & ALMOND SMOOTHIES

SERVES: 2

Ingredients

500 ml (2 cups) unsweetened almond milk
1 avocado, peeled and chopped
120 ml (½ cup) crushed ice
Freshly squeezed juice of 1 lime + 2 slices of lime, to garnish
Hot paprika, to dust

Special Tip: *Unsweetened almond milk is a low-calorie beverage rich in heart-healthy fats. A cup contains just 30 calories, less than 1 gram of carbohydrates, and will cause little, if any, increase in blood sugar.*

Method:

195 CALORIES

Place two tall glasses in the freezer to chill while you prepare the smoothies.

Combine the almond milk, avocado, ice and lime juice in a blender and blend until smooth.

Pour into the glasses. Garnish with the lime, dust with the paprika, and serve.

BERRY CHIA SEED PUDDINGS

SERVES: 4

Ingredients

500 ml (2 cups) unsweetened almond milk
½ teaspoon vanilla essence (extract)
½ cup chia seeds
1 tablespoon maple syrup
1 teaspoon ground cinnamon
150 g (1 cup) fresh berries, such as blueberries or raspberries, to serve

Special Tip: *These puddings can be prepared the night before and set aside to chill. They are very nutritious and will set you up perfectly for the busiest of days.*

Method:

160 CALORIES

Whisk the almond milk, vanilla, chia seeds and maple syrup in a bowl. Let sit for 5–10 minutes and then whisk again to stop the seeds from clumping.

Cover and chill for 4 hours, or overnight.
Stir the mixture once or twice during chilling.

Spoon the pudding mixture into four serving glasses or bowls. Top with the berries, and serve.

YOGHURT & FRUIT CUP

SERVES: 3

Ingredients

500 ml (2 cups) plain Greek yoghurt
2 tablespoons ground flaxseed
3 peeled kiwifruit or peaches, coarsely chopped with a knife
1 tablespoon flaked almonds, to garnish

Special Tip:

Thick creamy Greek yoghurt is strained to remove liquid whey. This process increases the amount of protein per serving and also removes some of the carbohydrates.

Method:

250 CALORIES

Mix the yoghurt, flaxseed and fruit in a bowl or jug (pitcher).

Pour into three serving glasses. Sprinkle with the almonds, and serve.

PANCAKES WITH BLUEBERRIES

Ingredients

- 2 large free-range eggs
- 50 g (⅓ cup) self-rising flour
- 50 g (⅓ cup) old-fashioned oats
- 4 teaspoons Splenda sweetener
- 1 teaspoon ground cinnamon
- 150 ml (⅔ cup) unsweetened soya or almond milk
- Cooking spray
- 150 g (1 cup) fresh blueberries

Special Tip:

Be sure to choose old fashioned or steel cut oats to make these pancakes as they have a much lower GI index than instant oats. This recipe will make 12–16 small pancakes, easily enough for four people.

Method:

125 CALORIES

Whisk the egg whites in a bowl until stiff peaks form. Beat the egg yolks, flour, oats, 2 teaspoons of Splenda, cinnamon and milk in a separate bowl until well mixed.

Gently fold the egg whites into the flour mixture.

Place a large frying pan over medium heat and spray lightly with cooking spray. Drop tablespoons of the pancake batter into the frying pan to make small pancakes.

Cook until puffed up, 3–4 minutes, then turn and cook on the other side until golden. Place the warm pancakes on a plate and keep warm, whilst you cook the others.

Meanwhile, warm the blueberries with 1–2 tablespoons of water and the remaining 2 teaspoons of Splenda in a small saucepan over medium-low heat. Simmer until softened.

Serve the pancakes warm with the blueberry sauce spooned over the top.

CREPES WITH RASPBERRIES

SERVES: 4

Ingredients

- 50 g (⅓ cup) wholemeal (whole-wheat) flour
- 1 tablespoon ground flaxseed
- ⅛ teaspoon sea salt
- 250 ml (1 cup) skimmed milk
- 3 large free-range eggs
- 1 teaspoon vanilla essence (extract)
- 1 teaspoon canola or sesame oil
- 300 g (2 cups) fresh raspberries
- Ground cinnamon, to dust

Special Tip:

This recipe makes four medium-size crepes, enough to serve four. This makes a wonderful lazy weekend brunch to share with friends and family.

Method:

180 CALORIES

Combine the flour, flaxseed and salt in a bowl. Whisk the milk, eggs and vanilla in a separate bowl until well mixed. Stir into the flour mixture and whisk until smooth. Let the batter stand at room temperature for 15 minutes.

Brush a medium frying pan with the oil and place over medium heat. Pour in about 2 tablespoons of the batter, swirling the pan to cover the bottom. Cook until firm and golden, 2–3 minutes. Flip and cook for 30 seconds on the other side.

Combine the raspberries and cinnamon in a bowl and mash coarsely with a fork.

Serve the pancakes hot with the raspberry mixture spooned over the top.

MEXICAN EGGS

Ingredients

- 4 large free-range eggs
- ¼ teaspoon ground cumin
- ¼ teaspoon chilli powder
- Sea salt & black pepper
- 1 tablespoon olive oil
- 1 (400-g/14-ounce) can black beans, drained & rinsed
- 1 medium tomato, diced
- 1 small red onion, finely chopped
- 50 g (1 cup) fresh spinach
- 1 ripe avocado, peeled, pitted & coarsely mashed with a fork
- 6 tablespoons fresh salsa (see page 37)

Special Tip:

This hearty dish has quite a high calorie count and is best served as brunch (ie when you are skipping lunch). It has enough fibre and healthy fats to keep you feeling full for hours.

Method:

390 CALORIES

Whisk the eggs in a bowl with the cumin, chilli powder, salt and pepper.

Heat the oil in a large frying pan over medium heat. Add the onion and sauté until softened, 3–4 minutes. Pour in the egg mixture and cook and stir for 1 minute.

Add the beans and tomato, and continue stirring until the eggs are almost ready. Stir in the spinach and cook until the eggs are cooked to your liking.

Divide the scrambled eggs evenly among three serving plates. Top with dollops of salsa and mashed avocado, and serve hot.

SPINACH & CHEESE BAKE

SERVES: 4

Ingredients

- 250 g (5 cups) spinach
- 250 g (1 cup) ricotta cheese
- 120 g (4 ounces) feta cheese, crumbled
- 4 scallions (spring onions), sliced
- 2 tablespoons chopped fresh dill
- 2 tablespoons chopped fresh chives
- ⅛ teaspoon freshly grated nutmeg
- 2 large free-range eggs, beaten
- Sea salt & black pepper

Special Tip:

This attractive dish can also be served for lunch or dinner. Add a green or mixed salad, and you're good to go!

Method:

250 CALORIES

Preheat the oven to 200°C (400°F/gas 6). Butter a 20-cm (8-inch) springform pan.

Rinse the spinach thoroughly in cold running water. Cook in a medium saucepan with just the water left clinging to the leaves until wilted, 1–2 minutes. Drain well. Squeeze the spinach to remove any excess water. Use a large knife to chop it coarsely on a chopping board.

Mix the ricotta, feta, scallions, dill, chives, nutmeg, eggs, and spinach in a large bowl. Season with salt and pepper.

Spoon the mixture into the prepared pan. Bake for about 20 minutes, until firm and cooked through.

Cut into four slices, and serve warm.

MINI SPINACH FRITTATAS

SERVES: 4

Ingredients

- 1 tablespoon olive oil
- 1 small red onion, finely chopped
- 2 cloves garlic, minced
- 350 g (7 cups) fresh spinach
- 6 large free-range eggs
- ¼ teaspoon sea salt
- ¼ teaspoon black pepper
- ¼ teaspoon nutmeg

Special Tip: *These delicious little frittatas are great for breakfast or brunch. If liked, serve them with a dash of sweet chilli sauce on top.*

Method:

165 CALORIES

Preheat the oven to 200°C (400°F/gas 6). Lightly oil eight cups of a standard muffin pan with oil.

Rinse the spinach throughly under cold running water. Cook with just the water left clinging to the leaves until just wilted, 1–2 minutes. Drain, squeezing out as much of the moisture as possible. Chop coarsely with a large knife on a chopping board.

Place the oil in a large frying pan over medium heat. Add the onion and sauté until softened, 3–4 minutes. Stir in the garlic and spinach. Cook for 1 minute. Remove from the heat and set aside to cool slightly.

Meanwhile, whisk the eggs, salt, pepper and nutmeg in a large bowl. Stir in the vegetable mixture.

Spoon the frittata mixture evenly into the greased muffin cups. Bake for 16-18 minutes, until puffed and golden. Remove from pan and serve hot.

SCRAMBLED EGGS & BAKED TOMATOES

Ingredients

8 medium vine tomatoes
1 tablespoon olive oil
Sea salt & black pepper
8 medium free-range eggs
60 ml (¼ cup) light (single) cream
1 tablespoon butter
2 tablespoons finely chopped fresh chives

Special Tip:

Tomatoes are a good source of lycopene which is believed to support bone health as well as to help protect against cardiovascular disease and some types of cancer. Cooking tomatoes increases the amount of lycopene available.

Method:

300 CALORIES

Preheat the oven to 180°C (350°F/gas 4).

Arrange the tomatoes in a single layer in a large roasting pan. Drizzle with the oil and season with salt and pepper. Bake for about 20 minutes, until the tomatoes are softened.

Meanwhile, beat the eggs with the cream in a large bowl until frothy.

Melt the butter in a large frying pan over medium heat. Add the egg mixture and cook, stirring often, until large chunks form, about 5 minutes.

Sprinkle with the chives and season with salt and pepper. Serve the eggs hot with the tomatoes on the side.

COURGETTE HASHED BROWNS

SERVES: 2

Ingredients

- 400 g (2 cups) coarsely grated courgettes (zucchini)
- 4 medium free-range eggs, lightly beaten
- 1 small onion, finely chopped
- 1 clove garlic, finely chopped
- 2 tablespoons finely chopped fresh parsley
- Sea salt & black pepper
- 1 tablespoon olive oil
- Tomato ketchup, to serve (optional)

Special Tip:

You can serve these delicious courgette hashed browns for breakfast, brunch, lunch or dinner. They are always a treat.

Method:

250 CALORIES

Combine the courgettes, eggs, onion, garlic and parsley in a large bowl. Season with salt and pepper and mix well.

Heat ½ tablespoon of oil in a large frying pan over medium-high heat. Add half the courgette mixture, spreading it to an even thickness.

Cook until browned, then flip and cook the other side, about 5 minutes each side.

Slice onto a plate. Cook the remaining courgette mixture in the same way. Serve warm, with the ketchup, if liked.

PESTO SCRAMBLE WITH MUSHROOMS

Ingredients

- 8 medium free-range eggs
- 60 ml (¼ cup) light (single) cream
- 1 tablespoon butter
- 2 tablespoons basil pesto
- 60 g (½ cup) freshly grated Parmesan
- Sea salt & black pepper
- 250 g (8 ounces) button mushrooms, thinly sliced
- 2 tablespoons finely chopped fresh parsley
- 1 tablespoon olive oil

Special Tip:

This tasty dish makes a great weekend brunch, providing enough energy and keeping hunger pangs at bay for hours.

Method:

375 CALORIES

Beat the eggs and cream in a large bowl.

Melt the butter in a large frying pan over medium heat. Add the egg mixture and cook, stirring often, until the eggs form large chunks, about 5 minutes. Stir in the pesto.

Spoon the scrambled eggs onto warmed serving plates. Sprinkle with the Parmesan. Season with salt and pepper.

Meanwhile, sauté the mushrooms and parsley in the oil in a large frying pan over medium heat until softened, about 5 minutes.

Serve the eggs hot with the mushrooms.

APPETIZERS & SNACKS

Here you will find a small selection of delicious ideas for appetizers and snacks. During the intensive first six weeks of this diet there won't be too many opportunities for snacking, but as your blood sugar levels return to normal and you reach your weight goals you can gradually increase your calorie intake.

CARROT & GRAPEFRUIT ZINGER

SERVES: 2

Ingredients

- 2 carrots
- 2 grapefruit, peeled and cut into segments
- 1 (2.5-cm/1-cm) piece fresh ginger, peeled and chopped
- 120 ml (½ cup) crushed ice

Special Tip:

Fresh carrot and grapefruit juice with ginger is very light and refreshing.

Method:

40 CALORIES

Place two serving glasses in the freezer to chill while you juice the carrots and grapefruit.

Juice the carrots, grapefruit and ginger into a jug (pitcher). Mix well.

Divide the ice evenly between the two chilled glasses. Pour the juice in over the top. Serve immediately.

AVOCADO JUICE WITH WASABI

SERVES: 2

Ingredients

- ½ iceberg lettuce
- 2 limes, peeled
- 1 medium cucumber, peeled & seeded
- 1 avocado, peeled and pitted
- 2 teaspoons wasabi
- 8–10 ice cubes

Special Tip:

The wasabi adds a delicious zing to the flavour of this healthy juice.

Method:

190 CALORIES

Juice the lettuce, limes and cucumber into a jug (pitcher).

Reserve a few small cubes of avocado. Combine the remaining avocado with the juice and wasabi in a blender and blend until smooth.

Divide the ice cubes between two medium glasses and pour the avocado mixture in over the top. Top with the reserved cubes of avocado, and serve.

KALE CHIPS

SERVES: 6

Ingredients

- 300 g (6 cups) curly kale, preferably organic
- 2 tablespoons olive oil
- 1 tablespoon fresh lemon juice
- 1 teaspoon garlic powder
- 1 teaspoon onion powder
- ½ teaspoon chilli powder
- ½ teaspoon sea salt flakes
- ¼ teaspoon cayenne pepper

Special Tip:

With more than 45 different flavonoids, kale is one of nature's superfoods. It will help to detoxify your body and reduce inflammation.

Method:

70 CALORIES

Preheat the oven to 150°C (300°F/gas 2). Line a large rimmed baking sheet with parchment paper.

Remove the leaves from the stems of the kale and tear into large pieces. Rinse the leaves thoroughly and dry on a clean kitchen cloth.

Put the kale leaves into a large bowl. Drizzle with the oil, massaging with your fingertips to make sure it coats the leaves all over.

Sprinkle with the lemon juice, garlic powder, onion powder, chilli powder, salt and pepper, tossing to combine.

Spread the kale out on the prepared baking sheet in a single layer. Don't overcrowd it. Make a second baking sheet if required.

Bake for 10 minutes, rotate the pan, then bake for about 15 minutes more, until the kale starts to become crisp and slightly wilted. Serve warm.

FRESH SALSA

Ingredients

- 3 medium salad tomatoes, finely chopped
- 2 cloves garlic, minced
- 2 fresh red chillies, seeded & finely chopped
- 1 small sweet red onion, finely chopped
- 3 tablespoons finely chopped fresh coriander (cilantro)
- Freshly squeezed juice of 1 lime
- Sea salt & black pepper

Special Tip:

This Mexican and Tex-Mex classic is easy and quick to prepare and very low in calories and carbs. Serve as a dip with strips of red pepper, or spoon a dollop onto some of the meat or fish dishes in this book.

Method:

41 CALORIES

Put the tomatoes in a medium bowl and add the garlic, chillies, onion, cilantro and lime juice. Season with salt and pepper.

Cover and chill for at least 30 minutes before serving.

PUMPKIN HUMMUS

Ingredients

- 350 g (12 ounces) pumpkin
- 1 (400-g/14-ounce) can chickpeas (garbanzo beans), drained & rinsed
- 2 cloves garlic, minced
- 1 teaspoon ground cumin
- 1 teaspoon ground coriander
- 2 tablespoons tahini
- 1 tablespoon olive oil
- 1 tablespoon fresh lemon juice
- Sea salt flakes
- 2 tablespoons pumpkin seeds
- Celery sticks, to serve

Special Tip:

The pumpkin in this tasty hummus turns the dish an eye-catching orange colour, making it a feast for the eyes as well as the palate.

Method:

190 CALORIES

Steam the pumpkin until tender, about 10 minutes. Drain and let cool to room temperature.

Combine the pumpkin, chickpeas, garlic, cumin, coriander, tahini, oil and lemon juice in the bowl of a food processor and chop until smooth. Season with salt to taste.

Spoon the hummus into a serving bowl. Sprinkle with the pumpkin seeds and serve with the celery.

GUACAMOLE HUMMUS

SERVES: 6

Ingredients

- 1 (400-g/14-ounce) can chickpeas (garbanzo beans), drained and rinsed
- 150 g (3 cups) fresh coriander (cilantro) leaves
- 2 cloves garlic, chopped
- 1 ripe avocado, pitted & chopped
- 2 tablespoons olive oil
- 1 tablespoon fresh lime juice
- Sea salt & black pepper
- 1 small red chilli, seeded & thinly sliced
- Cucumber & red pepper (capsicum) sticks, to serve

Special Tip:

This delicious mixture of two favourite dips combines the flavours and health benefits of them both.

Method:

150 CALORIES

Combine the chickpeas, coriander, garlic and avocado in a food processor and chop until smooth.

With the machine running, add the oil in a slow, steady stream, then add the lime juice. If the mixture is too thick, add a little extra lime juice or water. Season with salt and pepper.

Spoon into a dish and garnish with the chilli. Serve with the cucumber and red pepper sticks.

WARM CANNELLINI DIP WITH CRUDITÉS

SERVES: 8

Ingredients

1 bulb garlic
250 ml (1 cup) unsweetened almond milk
2 (400-g/14-ounce) cans cannellini beans, drained & rinsed
2 tablespoons olive oil
1½ tablespoons white wine vinegar
1 teaspoon fresh thyme + extra, to garnish
Crudités (radishes, broccoli florets, baby carrots, cauliflower florets), to serve

Special Tip:

Cannellini beans are a superb source of manganese and dietary fibre. They are also rich in other elements, including magnesium, potassium, iron, folate, calcium and protein.

Method:

115 CALORIES

Preheat the oven to 190°C (375°F/gas 5). Put the garlic in a small roasting pan and bake for 30 minutes, until tender when pierced with a skewer or the point of a sharp knife.

Remove the garlic from the oven and carefully squeeze the flesh out of each clove into a small pan.

Add the almond milk, beans, oil, vinegar and thyme, bring to a boil over medium heat, then simmer on low for 10 minutes.

Remove from the heat and purée in a food processor or using a hand-held blender until smooth. Return to the pan and heat through.

Arrange the crudités on a large serving platter. Transfer the dip to a large heatproof bowl and place in the center of the larger platter. Garnish with the thyme and serve warm with the crudités.

PEA & PARMESAN DIP

Ingredients

- 450 g (3 cups) frozen peas
- 500 ml (2 cups) vegetable stock
- 2 cloves garlic, peeled
- 3 tablespoons pine nuts
- 120 g (1 cup) freshly grated Parmesan cheese
- ¼ cup finely chopped fresh mint
- 2 tablespoons olive oil
- Sea salt & black pepper
- Crudités (radishes, broccoli florets, baby carrots, cauliflower florets), to serve

Special Tip:

The slightly sweet flavour of the peas and mint in this dip makes a delicious change from the usual pre-dinner dips.

Method:

165 CALORIES

Put the peas in a pan with the stock and cook over medium heat until bright green and just tender, 3–4 minutes. Remove from the heat.

Reserve 1 cup of peas and transfer the rest to a food processor with the garlic. Chop with just enough of the cooking liquid to make a smooth purée. Place the purée in a bowl and stir in reserved peas.

Toast the pine nuts in a small frying pan over medium heat. Chop coarsely and stir into the pea mixture.

Stir in the Parmesan, mint, and oil. Season with salt and pepper. Serve with the crudités.

MIXED SALAD

Ingredients

200 g (4 cups) mixed baby salad greens
20 cherry tomatoes, halved
1 red pepper (capsicum), cored & sliced
1 cucumber, sliced
Small bunch fresh basil, coriander (cilantro) or mint, chopped
Freshly squeezed juice of 1 lemon or lime
Sea salt & pepper

Special Tip:

This salad makes a delicious snack or very light meal. With just 40 calories per serving, you can also serve it with many of the lunch and dinner dishes in the next two chapters.

Method:

40 CALORIES

Combine the salad greens, cherry tomatoes, red pepper, cucumber and herbs in a large salad bowl.

Drizzle with the lemon or lime juice and season with salt and pepper. Toss gently, and serve.

COLESLAW

SERVES: 4

Ingredients

200 g (4 cups) coarsely grated Savoy or white cabbage
1 medium apple, cored and coarsely grated
2 medium carrots, coarsely grated
1 small sweet red onion, grated
½ cup finely chopped fresh parsley
120 ml (½ cup) plain yoghurt
2 teaspoons cider vinegar
2 teaspoons Dijon mustard
Sea salt & black pepper

Special Tip:

This is another great salad to snack on or to serve as an appetizer or side dish with some of the meat and fish dishes in the lunch and dinner chapters. For extra freshness and flavour, add 1 small grated fresh fennel bulb.

Method:

75 CALORIES

Combine the cabbage, apple, carrots, onion and parsley in a large bowl, tossing well to mix.

Whisk the yoghurt, vinegar and mustard in a separate bowl. Season with salt and pepper.

Pour the dressing over the coleslaw. Toss well so that the vegetables are well coated.

Cover the bowl with plastic wrap and chill for 1–2 hours before serving.

LIGHT LUNCHES

In this chapter we have focused on a selection of light and healthy dishes that are ideal for a midday meal. Most of us are busy during the day so we have chosen simple dishes, many of which can be prepared ahead of time. The soups can all be reheated, the gazpachos can stay in the refrigerator, while most of the salads can be thrown together in just a few minutes.

FIERY GAZPACHO

SERVES: 4

Ingredients

- 2 tablespoons red wine vinegar
- 12 medium vine tomatoes, peeled, seeded & chopped
- 1 red pepper (capsicum), seeded & coarsely chopped
- 1 fresh red chilli, chopped
- 1 tablespoon tomato paste
- 1 teaspoon chilli paste
- 2 tablespoons olive oil
- 250–500 ml (1–2 cups) iced water
- Sea salt & black pepper
- 4 green pickled chillies, sliced
- 2 tablespoons pitted black olives
- 1 tablespoon snipped chives

Special Tip:

The traditional recipe for gazpacho includes soaked bread which gives the soup its characteristic texture. But you can easily leave the bread out and still enjoy a delicious chilled soup on hot summer days.

Method:

125 CALORIES

Combine the vinegar, tomatoes, red pepper, chilli, tomato paste, chilli paste, and oil in the bowl of a food processor and chop until smooth.

Stir in enough of the water to make a thick soup; add more or less according to taste. Season with salt and pepper.

Cover the bowl with plastic wrap (cling film) and chill in the coldest part of the refrigerator for at least 4 hours.

Ladle the gazpacho into serving bowls or glasses, and top with the pickled chillies and olives. Sprinkle with the chives, and serve.

GREEN GAZPACHO

Ingredients

- 2 cloves garlic, peeled
- 1 large green pepper (capsicum)
- 1 green chilli, chopped
- 2 stalks celery
- 2 spring onions (scallions)
- 250 g (5 cups) spinach leaves
- 100 g (1 cup) blanched almonds
- 1 cucumber, diced
- 3 tablespoons sherry vinegar
- 2 tablespoons olive oil
- ½ cup fresh parsley
- 1 tablespoon fresh mint
- Sea salt & black pepper
- 120 ml (½ cup) crushed ice

Special Tip:

We have replaced the bread in this green gazpacho with one cup of nutritious almonds. Serve this soup well chilled on hot summer days.

Method:

234 CALORIES

Combine the garlic, green pepper, chilli, celery, spring onions, spinach, almonds, three-quarters of the cucumber, sherry vinegar, oil, parsley and mint in a food processor and chop to a coarse purée. If necessary, add a little extra cold water to get the perfect thick and smooth consistency. Season with salt and pepper.

Pour into a bowl. Cover the bowl with plastic wrap (cling film) and chill in the coldest part of the refrigerator for at least 4 hours.

Add the crushed ice to the soup and ladle into serving bowls or glasses. Sprinkle with the remaining cucumber, and serve.

CREAM OF MUSHROOM SOUP

SERVES: 6

Ingredients

- 1.5 kg (3 pounds) brown mushrooms, peeled, stalks removed, quartered (reserve the peelings and stalks)
- 6 shallots, 4 sliced, 2 whole
- 4 cloves garlic, peeled but whole
- 2 bay leaves
- 6 sprigs fresh thyme
- 2 litres (8 cups) vegetable stock
- 2 tablespoons olive oil
- 3 stalks celery, chopped
- 1 leek, sliced
- Sea salt & black pepper
- 6 tablespoons plain yoghurt

Special Tip:

Low in calories and cholesterol-free, mushrooms also provide a range of important nutrients, including selenium, potassium, riboflavin, niacin, vitamin D and more.

Method:

160 CALORIES

Combine the mushroom peelings and stalks, 2 whole shallots, 2 cloves garlic, bay leaves and thyme in a saucepan. Add the vegetable stock, bring to a boil, then simmer on low heat for 30 minutes.

Remove from the heat and strain through a fine-mesh sieve, discarding the solids. Set the stock aside.

Heat the oil in a soup pot over medium heat. Add the remaining shallots and garlic, celery, and leek and sauté until softened, 3–4 minutes. Season with salt and pepper.

Add the mushrooms and cook for 5 minutes. Pour in the reserved mushroom stock, bring to a boil, then simmer until the mushrooms are tender, about 20 minutes.

Purée the soup in a food processor or using a handheld blender. Gently reheat, without bringing to a boil.

Ladle into serving bowls and stir 1 tablespoon of yoghurt into each dish. Serve hot.

CREAM OF TOMATO SOUP WITH BASIL

SERVES: 4

Ingredients

2 tablespoons olive oil
6 shallots, thinly sliced
3 cloves garlic, finely chopped
2 bay leaves
1 bunch fresh basil, leaves & stalks separated, stalks tied with kitchen string
Sea salt & black pepper
2 (400-g/14-ounce) cans tomatoes, chopped, with juice
750 ml (3 cups) vegetable stock
1 teaspoon brown sugar
3 tablespoons water
4 tablespoons yoghurt

Special Tip:

This is a very low-calorie soup. Prepare it on days when you want to have a really light lunch.

Method:

115 CALORIES

Heat the oil in a soup pot over medium heat. Add the shallots, garlic, bay leaves and basil stalks, season with salt and pepper, and simmer for 5 minutes.

Add the tomatoes, vegetable stock and sugar, bring to a boil, then simmer for 20 minutes. Discard the basil stalks.

Remove from the heat and purée in a food processor or using a handheld blender. Add the basil leaves and water and pulse for 2 minutes.

Return the soup to the pan and reheat on low. Ladle into serving bowls, spoon a tablespoon of yoghurt into each bowl, and serve immediately.

SPICY LENTIL SOUP

SERVES: 4

Ingredients

- 2 tablespoons butter
- 2 teaspoons ground cumin
- 2 teaspoons black mustard seeds
- 1 teaspoon red pepper flakes
- ½ teaspoon turmeric
- 6 curry leaves
- 1 onion, finely chopped
- 2 cloves garlic, finely chopped
- 1 teaspoon minced ginger
- 1 carrot, diced
- 100 g (1½ cups) diced pumpkin
- Sea salt & black pepper
- 200 g (1 cup) red lentils
- 1.5 litres (6 cups) vegetable stock
- 100 g (2 cups) spinach
- Coriander (cilantro), to garnish

Special Tip:

Lentils are full of dietary fibre which not only helps lower cholesterol, but also prevents blood sugar levels rising rapidly after a meal.

Method:

300 CALORIES

Heat the butter in a soup pot over medium heat. Add the cumin, black mustard, red pepper flakes, turmeric and curry leaves and sauté for 30 seconds.

Add the onion, garlic, ginger, carrot and pumpkin, season with salt and pepper, and sauté for 5 minutes.

Add the lentils and vegetable stock, bring to a boil, then simmer until the lentils are soft and starting to break up, 25–30 minutes. Stir in the spinach leaves.

Ladle into serving bowls, garnish with the coriander, and serve hot.

SPICY BEEF SOUP

Ingredients

- 2 tablespoons olive oil
- 1 large onion, finely chopped
- 2 cloves garlic, finely chopped
- 1 carrot, finely chopped
- 1 stalk celery, finely chopped
- 1 fresh red chilli, finely chopped
- 2 tablespoons chopped parsley
- 350 g (12 ounces) lean minced (ground) beef
- 2 (400-g/14-ounce) cans tomatoes
- 1 litre (4 cups) beef stock
- Sea salt & black pepper
- 2 tablespoons coriander (cilantro), to garnish

Special Tip:

Make sure you use good quality lean beef for this soup. You want the protein but not too much extra fat.

Method:

275 CALORIES

Heat the oil in a large soup pot over medium-high heat. Add the onion, garlic, carrot, celery, chilli, and parsley and sauté until the onion is softened, about 5 minutes.

Add the beef and sauté until nicely browned, about 5 minutes.

Add the tomatoes, potatoes and beef stock. Season with salt and pepper. Partially cover the pan and simmer over medium-low heat until the potatoes are tender, 15–20 minutes.

Ladle into serving bowls, garnish with the coriander, and serve hot.

GRILLED HALLOUMI & ORANGE SALAD

SERVES: 4

Ingredients

50 g (½ cup) walnut halves
2 medium oranges
1 small bunch coarsely chopped fresh mint leaves
1 tablespoon white wine vinegar
2 tablespoons olive oil
Sea salt & black pepper
200 g (7 ounces) halloumi cheese, sliced into 8 pieces
200 g (4 cups) fresh watercress

Special Tip:

Halloumi cheese is made from a mixture of goat's and sheep's milk and it is especially good on the grill. Replace with another local white grilling cheese if it isn't readily available where you live.

Method:

300 CALORIES

Dry-fry the walnuts in a small frying pan over medium heat until crisp and toasted, 3–4 minutes. Set aside to cool.

Preheat a large grill pan (griddle) or frying pan over high heat.

Combine the segments of orange and juice, mint leaves, vinegar and oil in a large bowl. Season with salt and pepper and toss gently to mix.

Grill the cheese on both sides until charred and beginning to melt, 2–3 minutes each side.

Add the walnuts and watercress to the orange salad, tossing well. Top with the halloumi and season with black pepper. Serve warm.

BLUEBERRY, CHEESE & WALNUT SALAD

SERVES: 4

Ingredients

50 g (½ cup) walnut halves
400 g (8 cups) mixed salad greens
300 g (2 cups) fresh blueberries
150 g (5 ounces) blue cheese, such as Gorgonzola, Danish, Stilton or Roquefort, crumbled
½ cup coarsely chopped fresh parsley
2 tablespoons olive oil
3 tablespoons apple cider vinegar
1 clove garlic, minced
Sea salt and black pepper

Special Tip:

This light and refreshing salad makes an ideal light lunch.

Method:

325 CALORIES

Dry-fry the walnuts in a small frying pan over medium heat until crisp and toasted, 3–4 minutes. Set aside to cool.

Combine the salad greens, blueberries, cheese, and parsley in a salad bowl.

Whisk the oil, vinegar, garlic, salt and pepper in a small bowl.

Pour the dressing over the salad and toss gently to coat. Sprinkle with the walnuts, and serve.

CHICKEN & CHICKPEA SALAD

Ingredients

- 90 ml (⅓ cup) fresh lemon juice
- 3 cloves garlic, minced
- 2 tablespoons coarsely chopped fresh basil
- 1 teaspoon brown sugar
- 2 tablespoons olive oil
- Sea salt & black pepper
- 2 boneless skinless chicken breasts, sliced
- 1 (400-g/14-ounce) can chickpeas (garbanzo beans), drained & rinsed
- 200 g (4 cups) mixed baby salad greens

Special Tip:

This refreshing salad has plenty of protein and fibre to keep you going until dinnertime.

Method:

230 CALORIES

Whisk the lemon juice, garlic, basil, brown sugar and oil in a small bowl. Season with salt and pepper. Set aside.

Heat a grill pan (griddle) or barbecue over high heat. Grill the chicken until tender and cooked through, 3–5 minutes each side. During cooking, turn the chicken and baste with 2–3 tablespoons of the dressing.

Combine the chickpeas and salad greens in a salad bowl. Drizzle with the remaining dressing and toss gently.

Top with the chicken, toss a little, and serve.

CHICKEN, BRIE & WALNUT SALAD

Ingredients

2 boneless skinless chicken breasts
Pinch of mixed herbs
1 teaspoon sea salt flakes
1 pear, cored and thinly sliced, drizzled with 1 tablespoon fresh lemon juice
50 g (½ cup) walnut halves
120 g (4 ounces) blue cheese
100 g (2 cups) spinach leaves
2 tablespoons olive oil
4 tablespoons fresh lemon juice
1 clove garlic, minced
Black pepper

Special Tip:

Replace the spinach leaves with another salad green of your choice. Watercress, rocket (arugula) or lambs lettuce would all be good.

Method:

240 CALORIES

Bring 750 ml (3 cups) of water to a boil and add the mixed herbs, salt and chicken. Simmer until tender, 10–15 minutes. Let sit in the cooking water for 15 minutes. Drain well and set aside to cool.

Cut the chicken into 1-cm (½-inch) thick slices.

Toss the chicken, walnuts, pear, blue cheese and spinach in a salad bowl.

Whisk the oil, lemon juice, garlic, salt and pepper in a small bowl. Drizzle over the salad, toss gently, and serve.

TUNA SALAD WITH BEANS & EGGS

SERVES: 4

Ingredients

- 2 large free-range eggs
- 2 (400-g/14-ounce) cans white kidney beans, drained and rinsed
- 1 (350-g/12-ounce) can tuna, drained
- 50 g (½ cup) large black olives
- 2 tablespoons olive oil
- 2 tablespoons balsamic vinegar
- 1 tablespoon each finely chopped fresh mint & marjoram
- 2 tablespoons finely chopped fresh parsley + extra, to garnish
- Sea salt

Special Tip:

This nourishing salad can be prepared in just a few minutes. Be sure to rinse the beans under cold running water; this will reduce the amount of sodium (salt) they contain.

Method:

330 CALORIES

Bring the eggs to a boil in a small saucepan of water and boil for 7 minutes. Drain and rinse under cold running water. Shell the eggs and cut into wedges.

To prepare the dressing, whisk the oil, vinegar, mint, marjoram and parsley in a small bowl. Season with salt.

Put the beans in a large salad bowl and add the tuna and olives. Drizzle with the dressing and toss well.

Add the eggs. Garnish with the parsley, and serve.

GREEK CHICKEN SALAD

SERVES: 4

Ingredients

- 2 tablespoons plain yoghurt
- 3 tablespoons fresh lemon juice
- 1 tablespoon dried oregano
- 2 tablespoons chopped mint
- 500 g (1 pound) chicken tenderloins, trimmed
- 2 tablespoons olive oil
- 150 g (3 cups) spinach leaves
- 150 g (5 ounces) roasted yellow pepper (capsicum), from a jar
- 1 cucumber, coarsely chopped
- 120 g (4 ounces) feta cheese
- 50 g (½ cup) kalamata olives
- Sea salt & black pepper

Special Tip:

Serve this salad while the chicken is still warm. It makes a lovely lunch especially during the cold winter months.

Method:

290 CALORIES

Combine the yoghurt, 2 teaspoons of the lemon juice, oregano, and mint in a bowl, mixing well. Add the chicken, turning to coat. Cover and chill in the refrigerator for 30 minutes.

Preheat a grill pan (griddle), overhead grill (broiler) in the oven, or barbecue on medium heat.

Remove the chicken from the marinade and brush with the oil. Grill until cooked through, 5–10 minutes, depending on the cooking method.

Combine the spinach, yellow pepper, cucumber, feta and olives in a bowl. Toss to combine.

Divide the salad among four serving plates. Top each portion with a quarter of the chicken.

Drizzle with remaining lemon juice. Season with salt and pepper, and serve.

HERB FRITTATA WITH CREAM CHEESE

SERVES: 4

Ingredients

150 g (⅔ cup) cream cheese, softened
½ clove garlic, finely chopped
2 tablespoons chopped basil
¼ teaspoon Worcestershire sauce
6 medium free-range eggs
2 tablespoons milk
Sea salt & black pepper
30 g (¼ cup) freshly grated Parmesan cheese
1 tablespoon chopped thyme
1 tablespoon olive oil

Special Tip:

Serve this frittata with a simple green salad drizzled with a little freshly squeezed lemon juice.

Method:

290 CALORIES

Beat the cream cheese, garlic, basil and Worcestershire sauce in a small bowl until smooth. Set aside at room temperature.

Beat the eggs and milk in a large bowl. Season with salt and pepper. Stir in the Parmesan and thyme.

Heat ½ tablespoon of the oil in a large frying pan over medium heat. Pour in half the beaten egg mixture. Slide a wooden spatula under the eggs to loosen. Shake the pan with a rotating movement to spread.

Cook until nicely browned on the underside and firm on the top. Slip the frittata onto a serving plate and keep warm.

Add the remaining oil to the pan. Pour the remaining egg mixture into the pan and repeat the cooking process.

Spread the cream cheese mixture over the first frittata. Top with the second frittata. Slice into four wedges and serve hot.

TOMATO FRITTATA

SERVES: 4

Ingredients

3 medium vine tomatoes
½ teaspoon sea salt flakes
6 large free-range eggs
1 tablespoon tomato paste
6 sun-dried tomatoes, chopped
1 medium carrot, finely grated
½ bunch fresh chives, snipped
4 tablespoons chopped coriander (cilantro)
2 tablespoons chopped basil
150 g (5 ounces) mozzarella cheese, diced
1 tablespoon butter
60 g (½ cup) Parmesan flakes

Special Tip:

You can whip up this frittata in 10–15 minutes.

Method:

350 CALORIES

Finely chop the tomatoes and season with the salt. Let drain in a colander for 10 minutes.

Preheat the overhead grill (broiler) in the oven.

Beat the eggs in a large bowl and add the tomato paste, whisking until it has dissolved. Add the chopped tomatoes, sun-dried tomatoes, carrot, chives, cilantro, basil and mozzarella.

Melt the butter in a large frying pan over medium heat. Pour in the egg mixture. Cook over medium heat until nicely browned on the underside, about 5 minutes. Sprinkle with the Parmesan.

Grill the frittata about 5 inches (12 cm) from the heat source until the top is golden, 2–3 minutes. Cut into wedges and serve hot.

ROAST MUSHROOMS WITH BLUE CHEESE

SERVES: 4

Ingredients

- 2 tablespoons olive oil
- 10 large portobello mushrooms
- Sea salt & black pepper
- 350 g (7 cups) spinach leaves
- 1 onion, finely chopped
- 2 cloves garlic, minced
- 60 ml (¼ cup) dry sherry
- 120 g (4 ounces) blue cheese, crumbled
- 50 g (½ cup) coarsely chopped walnut pieces
- 60 g (½ cup) freshly grated Parmesan cheese

Special Tip:

Choose firm mushrooms all about the same size. When preparing them, just carefully wipe the tops with a damp cloth. Don't rinse them in cold water as they will absorb the water and release it again during cooking.

Method:

350 CALORIES

Preheat the oven to 225°C (450°F/gas 7). Place eight mushroom caps gill-side down in a large baking pan. Brush with 1 tablespoon of oil. Roast for 10–12 minutes, until tender. Remove from the oven, turn over, and season with salt and pepper.

Finely chop the remaining two mushroom caps and set aside.

Cook the spinach in a little lightly salted boiling water until wilted, 1–2 minutes. Drain well. Transfer to a clean kitchen cloth and squeeze out excess moisture. Coarsely chop with a knife.

Heat the remaining 1 tablespoon of oil in a large frying pan over medium heat. Add the onion and sauté until softened, 3–4 minutes. Add the chopped mushrooms and garlic and simmer for 3–4 minutes. Stir in the sherry and cook until it evaporates, 2–3 minutes. Add the spinach, blue cheese and walnuts and stir well.

Remove from the heat and spoon into the mushroom caps. Sprinkle with the Parmesan.

Bake for 10 minutes, until the topping is golden brown. Serve warm.

GRILLED COURGETTES WITH GOAT'S CHEESE

SERVES: 4

Ingredients

3 large courgettes (zucchini), sliced thinly lengthwise
2 tablespoons olive oil
1 tablespoon fennel seeds
Sea salt and black pepper
60 g (2 ounces) sliced bacon, rinds removed and chopped
1 large fennel bulb, thinly sliced
150 g (5 ounces) soft goat's cheese, crumbled
3 tablespoons fresh lemon juice
Fresh parsley, to garnish

Special Tip:

Courgettes are a very good source of potassium, an essential mineral which reduces blood pressure and heart rate by countering the effects of sodium.

Method:

315 CALORIES

Toss the courgettes in a bowl with 1 tablespoon of oil and the fennel seeds. Season with salt and pepper and set aside for 10 minutes.

Heat a grill pan (griddle) over medium-high heat and grill the courgettes for a few minutes on each side until tender.

Dry-fry the bacon in a large frying pan until crisp, about 5 minutes. Drain on kitchen paper.

Place the fennel in a large bowl and mix with the warm courgette, bacon and goat's cheese.

Whisk the lemon juice with the remaining tablespoon of oil. Season with salt and pepper and drizzle over the salad.

Garnish with the parsley, and serve.

PRAWNS WITH VEGETABLES

SERVES: 4

Ingredients

2 tablespoons olive oil
1 medium onion, finely chopped
1 red pepper (capsicum), diced
1 clove garlic, finely chopped
2 tomatoes, peeled and diced
100 g (2 cups) spinach
1 bunch asparagus, chopped
2 tablespoons dry white wine
3 tablespoons fresh lemon juice
Sea salt & black pepper
500 g (1 pound) raw prawns (shrimp), heads removed, shelled & deveined

Special Tip:

Prawns are an excellent source of high-quality protein. They are low in calories and contain no carbohydrates. These shellfish also contain heart-healthy, omega-3 fatty acids.

Method:

240 CALORIES

Heat 1 tablespoon of oil in a medium saucepan over medium heat. Add the onion and sauté until softened, 3–4 minutes. Add the red pepper, garlic and tomatoes and simmer for 7 minutes.

Stir in the spinach, asparagus, wine and lemon juice and season with salt and pepper. Cover and simmer gently until the spinach and asparagus are tender, about 5 minutes.

Meanwhile, heat the remaining 1 tablespoon of oil in a large frying pan over high heat. Add the prawns and sauté until pink and cooked through, 2–3 minutes.

Add the prawns to the vegetable mixture, stirring well. Serve hot.

WARM PRAWN & MONKFISH SALAD

SERVES: 4

Ingredients

- 2 tablespoons olive oil
- Sea salt & black pepper
- 1 tablespoon fresh lemon juice
- ½ teaspoon black pepper
- ½ teaspoon crushed fennel seeds
- ½ teaspoon red pepper flakes
- 250 g (8 ounces) monkfish fillets
- 16 jumbo prawns (shrimp), peeled & deveined
- 3 tablespoons sherry vinegar
- 1 tablespoon clarified butter
- 2 large tomatoes, peeled & diced
- 2 tablespoons chopped chervil
- 2 heads Belgian endive/chicory)

Special Tip: *Monkfish fillets are dense and do not flake and fall to bits as easily as many other types of white fish, making them ideal for soups and salads. If you can't get monkfish, replace it with cod in this recipe.*

Method:

200 CALORIES

Mix 1 tablespoon of oil, ½ teaspoon salt, lemon juice, peppercorns, fennel seeds and red pepper flakes in a shallow dish. Add the monkfish, turning to coat, and set aside to marinate for 1 hour.

Heat the remaining 1 tablespoon of oil in a large frying pan over high heat. Take the fish fillets out of the marinade and cook until lightly browned, 2 minutes on each side. Keep warm.

Add the prawns to the pan and toss over high heat until cooked through and lightly browned, about 2 minutes. Remove and keep warm.

Remove the pan from the heat and add the sherry vinegar and the marinade and let it bubble as the heat dissipates. Add the clarified butter, tomato and chervil. Season with salt and pepper.

Arrange the endive, fish and prawns on four serving plates and spoon the sherry and butter dressing over the top. Serve hot.

ASPARAGUS LOAF

Ingredients

- 500 g (1 pound) asparagus stalks, trimmed
- 1 courgette (zucchini), thinly sliced
- 6 tablespoons freshly grated Parmesan cheese
- Sea salt & black pepper
- 2 tablespoons butter, melted
- 6 large free-range eggs
- 120 ml (½ cup) light (single) cream
- Salad greens, to serve

Special Tip:

If asparagus is not in season, replace with the same weight of green beans.

Method:

310 CALORIES

Preheat the oven to 200°C (400°F/gas 6). Butter a large rectangular loaf pan.

Cook the asparagus in a large pot of salted boiling water until almost tender, 3–5 minutes. Drain and chop coarsely.

Arrange the asparagus and zucchini in layers in the prepared loaf pan. Sprinkle each layer with Parmesan and season with salt and pepper. Drizzle with the melted butter.

Beat the eggs and cream in a bowl until well blended. Pour the mixture over the vegetables.

Bake for 10–15 minutes, until firm and golden. Slice and serve hot or at room temperature with the salad greens.

GRILLED ASPARAGUS WITH EGG

SERVES: 4

Ingredients

750 g (1½ pounds) asparagus
1½ tablespoons red wine vinegar
5 tablespoons olive oil
2½ cloves garlic, minced
3 large free-range eggs
Handful of snipped fresh chives
1 teaspoon Dijon mustard
1 tablespoon white wine vinegar
Pinch of sugar
Sea salt & black pepper
3 tablespoons plain yoghurt

Special Tip:

This is a wonderful dish to serve in the spring and early summer when the new season's locally grown asparagus appears in the markets.

Method:

250 CALORIES

Cut off the woody ends of the asparagus. Place in a shallow bowl. Whisk the red vinegar, 2 tablespoons of oil, and 2 cloves of garlic in a bowl. Pour over the asparagus. Set aside for 20 minutes.

Put the eggs in a saucepan of cold water, bring to a boil, then simmer for 6 minutes. Refresh briefly under cold running water, and set aside.

Mix the remaining 3 tablespoons of oil into the mustard drop by drop. Thin with the white vinegar. Season with the garlic, sugar, salt and pepper, and stir in the yoghurt. Set aside.

Heat a grill pan (griddle) over medium-high heat and grill the asparagus until tender, 7–10 minutes, turning once or twice to cook evenly.

Reserve any excess marinade and pour into a small jug (pitcher) to serve.

Arrange the asparagus on a serving plate. Peel and chop the eggs. Pile on top of the asparagus. Drizzle with the mayonnaise and marinade and sprinkle with the chives. Serve warm.

DINNER

By dinnertime most of us are ready to relax after the stresses of the day. The last thing we need is an unhealthy readymade supermarket dinner. Here you will find a range of ideas for light and healthy meal thats will provide lots of nutrients and usher in a peaceful night's sleep. Do your shopping ahead of time so that your cupboards are always stocked with healthy, easy-to-prepare ingredients.

ROAST CAULIFLOWER WITH TOMATO SAUCE

SERVES: 4

Ingredients

2 tablespoons olive oil
1 head cauliflower, weighing about 1 kg (2 pounds), trimmed and cut in half
6 cloves garlic, finely chopped
½ cup fresh basil + extra leaves, to garnish
1 kg (2 pounds) tomatoes, peeled and coarsely chopped
60 ml (¼ cup) dry white wine + extra, as required
1 teaspoon red pepper flakes
Sea salt & black pepper

Special Tip:

For a slightly different dish, you could replace the cauliflower in this recipe with the same weight of broccoli.

Method:

180 CALORIES

Preheat the oven to 225°C (450°F/gas 7). Heat the oil in a large casserole with a lid. Add the cauliflower and brown over medium-high heat, about 5 minutes.

Set the cauliflower aside. Add the garlic and basil to the casserole and sauté until the garlic is golden, 2–3 minutes. Add the tomatoes, wine and red pepper flakes and season with salt and pepper. Stir well and bring to a simmer.

Return the cauliflower to the casserole. Baste with the tomato liquid and pile some of the solids on top. Simmer, uncovered, until the tomatoes reduce a little, about 5 minutes.

Cover the casserole, place in the oven, and roast for 30–40 minutes, until tender. Check on the tomato sauce every 10 minutes or so. Add extra wine if the sauce is too dry.

Divide the cauliflower and tomato sauce evenly among four serving plates. Garnish with basil, and serve hot.

GRILLED VEGETABLES WITH PECAN PESTO

Ingredients

- 5 tablespoons olive oil
- 4 medium courgettes (zucchini), thinly sliced lengthwise
- 1 red pepper (capsicum), seeded & cut into long strips
- 1 yellow pepper (capsicum), seeded & cut into long strips
- 1 large eggplant (aubergine), with peel, thinly sliced
- Sea salt & black pepper
- 50 g (½ cup) shelled pecans
- 100 g (2 cups) fresh parsley
- 3 cloves garlic
- ⅓ cup (40 g) grated Parmesan

Special Tip:

If you like some heat in your food, sprinkle the finished dish with red pepper flakes or thinly sliced fresh chilli.

Method:

315 CALORIES

Preheat a grill pan (griddle) over high heat. Brush with 1 teaspoon of oil. Place the zucchini in the pan and grill until tender and marked with brown lines, about 5 minutes each side.

Brush the pan with 1 teaspoon of oil. Place the bell pepper strips in the grill pan and grill until tender and marked with brown lines, about 10 minutes.

Brush the pan with 1 teaspoon of oil. Place the eggplant slices in the grill pan and grill until tender and marked with brown lines, about 5 minutes each side.

Combine all the grilled vegetables on a large serving plate. Season with salt and pepper.

Dry-fry the pecans in a small pan over medium heat until fragrant and crisp, 1–2 minutes.

Transfer the nuts to a food processor with the parsley, garlic, remaining 4 tablespoons of oil, and Parmesan and chop until smooth.

Serve the vegetables warm or at room temperature with the pecan pesto drizzled over the top.

SPICY VEGETABLE STEW

SERVES: 4

Ingredients

- 2 tablespoons peanut oil
- 1 teaspoon cumin seeds
- 1 large onion, thinly sliced
- 2 stalks celery, chopped
- 2 cloves garlic, finely chopped
- 1 red pepper (capsicum), sliced
- 2 courgettes (zucchini), sliced
- 1 aubergine (eggplant), diced
- 8 ounces (250 g) mushrooms
- 2 (400-g/14-ounce) cans tomatoes
- 1 teaspoon chilli powder
- 2 teaspoons ground coriander
- ½ teaspoon sea salt
- 1 (400-g/14-ounce) can red kidney beans, rinsed
- Fresh coriander (cilantro) leaves

Special Tip:

This is a warming dish to serve on cold winter days.

Method:

150 CALORIES

Heat the oil in a large saucepan over medium heat. Add the cumin seeds and toast until fragrant, about 2 minutes. Add the onion, celery and garlic and sauté until the onions are softened, about 5 minutes.

Add the peppers, courgettes, aubergine, mushrooms and tomatoes. Cover and simmer over medium heat until the vegetables begin to soften, about 5 minutes.

Add the chilli powder, coriander and salt. Mix well, then add the kidney beans. Cover and simmer until the vegetables are tender, 20–25 minutes. Stir occasionally during cooking.

Sprinkle with the coriander, and serve hot.

LENTIL STEW WITH PEPPERS

SERVES: 4

Ingredients

- 2 red peppers (capsicums), halved
- 2 tablespoons olive oil
- 1 large red onion, chopped
- 1 large carrot, diced
- 1 teaspoon paprika
- 200 g (1 cup) Le Puy lentils
- 1 clove garlic, sliced
- 4 ripe tomatoes, chopped
- 3 sprigs fresh thyme
- 2 bay leaves
- 500 ml (2 cups) vegetable stock
- 1 tablespoon capers
- 12 pitted black olives
- 2 tablespoons fresh parsley
- 2 tablespoons red wine vinegar
- Sea salt & black pepper

Special Tip: *Le Puy lentils are perfect in this stew as they don't become mushy during prolonged cooking.*

Method:

210 CALORIES

Preheat the overhead grill (broiler) in the oven. Grill the peppers skin-side up until blackened, about 10 minutes. Place in a plastic bag and tie the top. When cool enough to handle, peel off the skin. Cut into strips and set aside.

Heat the oil in a large saucepan over low heat. Add the onion and carrot. Cover and simmer until softened, about 10 minutes. Stir in the paprika.

Rinse the lentils under cold water and add to the saucepan with the garlic, tomatoes, thyme and bay leaves. Pour in enough of the stock to cover well. Increase the heat and bring to a boil, stirring frequently. Reduce the heat and simmer gently, uncovered, until the lentils are tender but not mushy, 20–25 minutes. Stir from time to time and check that there is enough cooking liquid, adding more stock if the stew looks dry.

Stir in the peppers, capers, olives and parsley. Remove the bay leaves and thyme, and stir in the vinegar. Cook for 10 more minutes.

Season with salt and pepper, and serve hot.

TOFU & LENTIL CURRY

SERVES: 4

Ingredients

1 tablespoon sesame oil	1 small cauliflower, in florets
1 onion, coarsely chopped	2 carrots, sliced
1 tablespoon finely grated ginger	1 large fresh red chilli, sliced
1 teaspoon ground turmeric	350 g (12 ounces) firm tofu, diced
2 teaspoons garam masala	250 g (8 ounces) green beans
600 ml (2½ cups) vegetable stock	Sea salt & black pepper
100 g (½ cup) red lentils	½ cup fresh coriander (cilantro)

Special Tip: *Tofu is a good source of calcium, protein, iron and a range of other minerals and phytonutrients. It is believed to help prevent heart disease and many types of cancer.*

Method:

210 CALORIES

Heat the oil in a large saucepan over medium heat. Add the onion and sauté until softened, 3–4 minutes. Stir in the ginger, turmeric, and garam masala and sauté until aromatic, about 1 minute.

Pour in the vegetable stock, lentils, cauliflower, carrots and chilli. Increase the heat to high and bring to a boil, then cover and simmer on low heat for 15 minutes.

Add the tofu and beans and simmer until all the vegetables are tender, about 10 minutes. Season with salt and pepper.

Stir in the coriander, and serve hot.

EGG & TOMATO CURRY

Ingredients

2 tablespoons sunflower oil
2 large onions, finely chopped
3 tablespoons tikka masala paste
1 (400-g/14-ounce) can chopped tomatoes, with juice
180 ml (¾ cup) water
Sea salt & black pepper
8 large free-range eggs
150 g (1 cup) frozen peas
6 tablespoons plain yoghurt
Fresh basil, to garnish

Special Tip:

This delicious light curry is quick and easy to prepare. It makes an ideal weeknight supper.

Method:

355 CALORIES

Heat the oil in a saucepan over medium-low heat. Add the onions and sauté until golden, 7–9 minutes. Add the tikka masala paste and sizzle for 2 minutes, stirring all the time.

Add the tomatoes and water, season with salt and pepper, and bring to a boil. Simmer until reduced, about 10 minutes.

Meanwhile, boil the eggs for 8 minutes, then cool in cold water. Peel and cut in half lengthwise.

Stir the peas and yoghurt into the curry sauce and simmer for 2–3 minutes. Add the eggs and simmer until heated through, 2–3 minutes.

Garnish with the basil, and serve hot.

SEAFOOD KEBABS WITH ANISEED SAUCE

SERVES: 4

Ingredients

- 2 tablespoons olive oil
- Grated zest and juice of 1 lemon
- Sea salt & black pepper
- 12 large prawns (shrimp), peeled, deveined & halved
- 350 g (12 ounces) tuna steak, cut into small chunks
- 120 ml (½ cup) single (light) cream
- 1 tablespoon Anisette liqueur
- ½ teaspoon sweet paprika
- 2 tablespoons finely chopped fresh dill
- 200 g (4 cups) salad greens

Special Tip:

Anisette, or Anis, is an aniseed-flavoured liqueur produced in many Mediterranean countries such as Spain, Italy and France. It goes beautifully with the cream and dill in the sauce for this dish.

Method:

375 CALORIES

Preheat the overhead grill (broiler) in the oven to medium-high.

Mix the oil, lemon zest and 1 tablespoon of the lemon juice in a small bowl. Season with salt and pepper.

Thread the prawns and tuna onto skewers and place them on a plate. Drizzle with the oil mixture.

Mix the cream, anisette, remaining lemon juice, paprika, and dill in a small bowl. Season with salt and pepper.

Grill the kebabs, turning them often, for 5 minutes, or until cooked through.

Arrange the salad greens on serving dishes and top with the kebabs. Drizzle with the sauce and serve hot.

BAKED SOLE WITH CHERRY TOMATOES

SERVES: 4

Ingredients

2 tablespoons olive oil
6 sole fillets, about 600 g (1¼ pounds) total weight
Sea salt & black pepper
500 g (1 pound) cherry tomatoes, halved
4 cloves garlic, finely chopped
2 tablespoons finely chopped fresh basil + extra leaves, to serve

Special Tip:

This attractive dish is high on nutrients and low in calories. It makes a nice light supper. Serve with a mixed salad, if liked (see page 40).

Method:

220 CALORIES

Preheat the oven to 180°C (350°F/gas 4). Grease a large baking dish with ½ tablespoon of the oil.

Arrange the sole in the prepared dish. Season with salt and pepper. Top with the tomatoes, garlic and basil. Season with salt and pepper. Drizzle with the remaining 1½ tablespoons of oil.

Bake for 10–15 minutes, until the sole is cooked and the tomatoes have softened. Sprinkle with the basil, and serve hot.

SEAFOOD SALAD

SERVES: 6

Ingredients

- 2 tablespoons coarse sea salt
- 1 stalk celery
- 1 bunch fresh parsley + 4 tablespoons finely chopped
- 1 unwaxed lemon, quartered
- 400 g (14 ounces) baby octopus
- 400 g (14 ounces) calamari, sliced
- 400 g (14 ounces) prawns (shrimp), heads removed
- 400 g (14 ounces) each clams & mussels, in shell, cleaned
- 3 tablespoons olive oil
- 4 cloves garlic, minced
- 1 teaspoon red pepper flakes
- 3 tablespoons fresh lemon juice
- Sea salt & black pepper

Special Tip:

This is a classic Italian recipe for seafood salad. It takes some time to prepare and is quite a special dish, which makes it ideal for special occasions.

Method:

320 CALORIES

Bring 2 litres (8 cups) of water to a boil over high heat. Add 1 tablespoon of coarse sea salt, the celery, bunch of parsley and lemon. Add the baby octopus and calamari. Return to a rapid boil and cook until white and tender, 3–5 minutes. Do not overcook. Drain and let cool. Place in a salad bowl.

Bring 1.5 litres (6 cups) of water and the remaining coarse salt to a boil. Add the prawns and cook for 2 minutes. Drain and let cool. Shell the prawns and add to the salad bowl.

Rinse the clams and mussels. Place in a large saucepan with 2 tablespoons of water, cover, and cook over medium heat until they are all open, 5–10 minutes. Discard any that have not opened. Discard the shells and add the clams and mussels to the salad bowl.

Mix the chopped parsley, garlic, red pepper flakes, lemon juice, oil, salt and pepper in a bowl. Pour over the salad and toss well.

Cover and chill in the refrigerator for at least 30 minutes before serving.

SPICY PRAWNS WITH ORANGE

Ingredients

2 tablespoons olive oil
6 cloves garlic, finely chopped
Finely grated zest of 1 unwaxed orange (orange part only)
1–2 small fresh red chillies, finely chopped
1 kg (2 pounds) prawns (shrimp), heads removed, peeled & deveined
Sea salt & black pepper
2 tablespoons finely chopped parsley

Special Tip:

This simple dish depends on the quality of the prawns. Buy them very fresh from a reliable fish vendor.

Method:

335 CALORIES

Heat the oil in a large frying pan and add 3 cloves of garlic, the orange zest, and chillies. Sauté over medium-high heat until the garlic is pale golden brown, 4–5 minutes.

Add the prawns and sauté for 3–4 minutes, until pink and cooked through. Season with salt and pepper and add the parsley and remaining garlic. Remove from the heat and serve hot.

COD WITH TOMATO & CAPER SAUCE

SERVES: 4

Ingredients

2 tablespoons olive oil
1 onion, finely chopped
3 cloves garlic, finely chopped
10 plum tomatoes, peeled & chopped
2 tablespoons capers, drained
750 g (1½ pounds) cod fillets
2 tablespoons finely chopped parsley
Sea salt

Special Tip:

Mild-flavoured and versatile, cod is available throughout the year. Try it in this easily prepared supper dish.

Method:

250 CALORIES

Heat the oil in a large frying pan over medium heat. Add the onion and garlic and sauté until softened, 3–4 minutes.

Add the tomatoes and simmer for 10 minutes to reduce the liquid a little. Add the capers and cook for 5 more minutes.

Rinse the cod fillets carefully and pat dry with paper towels. Season with salt and place in the tomato sauce. Reduce the heat and simmer gently until cooked, 8–10 minutes.

Sprinkle with the parsley, and serve hot.

ROAST SALMON WITH VEGETABLES

SERVES: 4

Ingredients

- 2 red peppers (capsicums), seeded & sliced into strips
- 2 bulbs fennel, outer leaves removed, cut into thin wedges
- 2 courgettes (zucchini), trimmed & cut into thick rounds
- 8 plum tomatoes
- 3 tablespoons olive oil
- 6–8 cloves garlic, cut in half
- 2–3 tablespoons fresh rosemary
- Sea salt & black pepper
- 600 g (1¼ pounds) salmon fillets

Special Tip:

Try to buy wild salmon for this dish. The meat is much tastier, leaner and richer in omega-3 fatty acids than farmed salmon.

Method:

375 CALORIES

Preheat the oven to 230°C (450°F/gas 8).
Put all the vegetables into a large baking dish, along with half the oil, half the garlic, half the rosemary, several pinches of salt and some black pepper. Toss the vegetables to coat well.

Roast 25–30 minutes, until the vegetables are about two-thirds cooked.

Push the vegetables to the side of the dish to make space for the fish. Arrange the salmon in a single layer. Mix the remaining oil, garlic, and rosemary in a bowl and pour over the fish. Season and bake for 10 minutes.

Use a spoon to scoop up some of the oil and juices at the bottom of the dish, and baste the fish and vegetables with it.

Return the dish to the oven and bake for 5–8 more minutes, depending on the thickness of the fish fillets.

Serve the salmon and vegetables hot with the cooking juices spooned over the top.

CHICKEN KEBABS WITH LEMON & HERBS

Ingredients

1 tablespoon chopped parsley
1 tablespoon chopped rosemary
2 teaspoons chopped thyme
1 clove garlic, minced
1 teaspoon black pepper
Finely grated zest & juice of 1 unwaxed lemon
1 teaspoon red chilli paste
3 tablespoons olive oil
2 boneless skinless chicken breasts, cut into small cubes
Lemon wedges, to serve
Mixed salad (see page 40), to serve

Special Tip:

A chicken breast is made up of two halves. Each half weighs about 150 g (5 ounces) and is enough for one serving.

Method:

350 CALORIES

Mix the parsley, rosemary, thyme, garlic, black pepper, lemon zest and juice, chilli paste and 2 tablespoons of oil in a medium bowl. Add the chicken, tossing well to coat. Set aside to marinate for 15 minutes.

Preheat a large grill pan (griddle) or barbecue on high heat.

Drain the chicken from the marinade, reserving the marinade. Thread the chicken onto skewers. Cook on the grill, turning and brushing often with the marinade, until tender and golden, about 10 minutes.

Serve hot with the green salad and lemon wedges.

GARLICKY GRILLED CHICKEN

SERVES: 4

Ingredients

- 2 tablespoons olive oil
- Finely grated zest and juice of 1 unwaxed lemon
- 4 cloves garlic, minced
- 2 tablespoons chopped parsley
- 2 boneless skinless chicken breasts, halved lengthwise
- Sea salt & black pepper
- 4 medium vine tomatoes, halved
- 200 g (4 cups) rocket (arugula) or other salad greens

Special Tip: *Chicken is a great source of protein and without the skin it is lean and healthy. Try to buy free-range or organic chicken, if you can afford it.*

Method:

350 CALORIES

Mix the oil, lemon zest and juice, garlic and parsley in a small dish. Season with salt and pepper. Add the chicken and coat well.

Preheat a grill pan (griddle) or barbecue on high heat.

Grill the chicken until golden and cooked through, 5–6 minutes on each side.

Season the tomatoes with salt and pepper and place cut-side down on the grill to soften, 3–4 minutes.

Divide the salad greens evenly among four serving plates. Top with the chicken and tomatoes, and serve hot.

CHICKEN & BROCCOLI STIR-FRY

Ingredients

4 teaspoons peanut oil
60 g (2 ounces) cashew nuts
600 g (1¼ pounds) boneless skinless chicken thighs
1 onion, cut into thin wedges
1 head broccoli, broken into florets
3 cloves garlic, finely chopped
120 ml (½ cup) Chinese oyster sauce
3 tablespoons soy sauce
Handful fresh coriander (cilantro), to serve

Special Tip:

You won't need to add any extra to salt to this dish because the oyster sauce and soy sauce are salty enough. If you like spicy food, add a finely chopped fresh red chilli along with the cashews at the end.

Method:

475 CALORIES

Heat 1 teaspoon of oil in a wok over high heat. Add the cashews and stir-fry until golden, 2–3 minutes. Transfer to a plate.

Heat 1 teaspoon of oil in the same wok over high heat. Stir-fry half the chicken until golden and almost cooked through, 3–4 minutes. Transfer to a plate. Heat another teaspoon of oil in the wok and cook the remaining chicken. Set aside.

Heat the remaining 1 teaspoon of oil in the wok. Add the onion and stir-fry until tender, about 2 minutes. Add the broccoli and garlic. Stir-fry until the broccoli is bright green, about 2 minutes.

Add the oyster sauce, soy sauce, and chicken to the wok. Stir-fry until hot. Add the cashews and toss well. Serve hot

CHICKEN WITH PEPPERS

Ingredients

1 tablespoon olive oil
2 cloves garlic, finely chopped
1 chicken, about 1.5 kg (3 pounds), cut into 8 pieces
Sea salt & black pepper
120 ml (½ cup) dry white wine
500 g (1 pound) firm, ripe tomatoes, peeled and chopped
3 medium mixed red, yellow & green peppers (capsicums), chopped into squares
½ cup fresh coriander (cilantro) leaves, to sprinkle

Special Tip:

This delicious chicken stew should be simmered over low heat until the meat and vegetables are very tender.

Method:

350 CALORIES

Heat the oil in a large frying pan over medium heat. Add the garlic and sauté until pale golden brown, 3–4 minutes.

Add the chicken pieces and sauté over medium-high heat until golden brown all over, about 5 minutes. Season with salt and pepper.

Pour in the wine and simmer until it has evaporated, 2–3 minutes. Add the tomatoes and peppers and simmer until the chicken and peppers are tender and the tomatoes have reduced, 35–40 minutes.

Sprinkle with the coriander, and serve hot.

CHICKEN WITH FETA & OLIVES

SERVES: 4

Ingredients

- 1 tablespoon olive oil
- 6 boneless chicken thighs, with skin, halved
- 2 red onions, thinly sliced
- 3 tablespoons fresh orange juice
- 2 tablespoons fresh lemon juice
- 50 g (1 cup) black olives
- 100 g (3½ ounces) feta cheese, crumbled
- 200 g (4 cups) salad greens, to serve

Special Tip:

The citrus juices help keep the chicken moist and tasty as it simmers in the pan. They also add delicious flavour.

Method:

400 CALORIES

Heat the oil in a large frying pan over medium-high heat. Sauté the chicken, turning once, until golden, about 10 minutes.

Add the onions and sauté until just tender, 3–4 minutes. Add the orange and lemon juice. Cover and bring to a simmer. Sprinkle with the olives and feta. Cover and cook for 1 minute.

Arrange the salad greens on serving plates. Top with the chicken and drizzle with the pan juices. Serve hot.

SPICED DUCK WITH ROASTED PUMPKIN

SERVES: 4

Ingredients

400 g (14 ounces) pumpkin (butternut squash), seeded & sliced 1 cm (½ inch) thick
2 tablespoons olive oil
Sea salt & black pepper
1 tablespoon soy sauce
1 teaspoon five-spice powder
4 boneless duck breast halves, with skin, about 400 g (14 ounces) total weight
2 tablespoons red wine vinegar
200 g (4 cups) salad greens, to serve

Special Tip:

Five-spice powder is a mixture of spices traditionally used in Chinese cuisine. The spices in the mix usually include cinnamon, cloves, fennel, star anise and szechuan pepper.

Method:

315 CALORIES

Preheat the oven to 220°C (425°F/gas 7). Place the pumpkin in a large baking pan and brush with 1 tablespoon of oil. Season with salt and pepper. Roast, turning once, until tender, about 15 minutes.

Meanwhile, combine the soy sauce and Chinese five-spice powder in a bowl. Brush the duck with this mixture.

Heat a frying pan over medium-high heat. Sauté the duck, skin-side down, until golden brown and crisp, about 5 minutes. Turn and sauté for 3–5 minutes, until cooked to your liking. Transfer to a plate, cover, and let rest for 5 minutes. Slice the duck.

Whisk the remaining 1 tablespoons of oil, vinegar, salt and pepper in a small bowl. Pour over the salad greens, tossing to combine.

Arrange the pumpkin and salad on serving plates. Top with the sliced duck, and serve hot.

VEAL SALTIMBOCCA WITH ASPARAGUS

SERVES: 4

Ingredients

8 small veal escalopes, about 600 g (1¼ pounds) total weight
2 tablespoons butter
8 very thin slices prosciutto, about 100 g (3½ ounces)
Bunch of fresh sage + 1 tablespoon coarsely chopped
Sea salt
60 ml (¼ cup) dry white wine
500 g (1 pound) fresh asparagus, steamed, to serve

Special Tip:

Enjoy this classic Italian veal dish with steamed asparagus or another green vegetable of your choice.

Method:

375 CALORIES

Lightly pound the veal with a meat tenderizer so that it is thin and of even thickness.

Melt the butter in a large frying pan over high heat. Cook the veal until browned, 2–3 minutes on each side. If the escalopes don't all fit in the pan in a single layer, cook them in two pans or in two batches.

Remove from the pan, top each escalope with a half slice of prosciutto and two sage leaves. Secure with toothpicks.

Return the veal to the pan with the butter and add the chopped sage. Cook over medium heat for 1 minute. Season with salt.

Turn up the heat. Pour in the wine and let it evaporate. Discard the toothpicks and serve at once with the asparagus.

VEAL ESCALOPES WITH ROCKET

SERVES: 4

Ingredients

8 small veal escalopes, about 600 g (1¼ pounds) total weight
Sea salt & black pepper
2 tablespoons olive oil
3 tablespoons balsamic vinegar
100 g (2 cups) rocket (arugula), coarsely chopped
100 g (3½ ounces) Parmesan cheese, shaved

Special Tip:

Cut from the topside or rump of young beef cattle, escalopes are very tender. They are lightly beaten to make them as thin as possible.

Method:

330 CALORIES

Lightly pound the veal with a meat tenderizer so that it is thin and of even thickness. Season the veal with salt and pepper.

Heat the oil in a large frying pan over high heat. Add the escalopes and brown on both sides, about 5 minutes (depending on the thickness of the meat).

Add the balsamic vinegar and simmer until it evaporates. Add the rocket and let it wilt for 1 minute.

Remove from the heat and let rest for 3 minutes. Sprinkle with the Parmesan and season with salt and pepper. Serve hot.

MEAT & VEGGIE SKEWERS

SERVES: 6

Ingredients

- 350 g (12 ounces) pork tenderloin
- 350 g (12 ounces) boned veal shoulder or shank
- 2 boneless skinless chicken breast halves
- 1 red pepper (capsicum)
- 1 yellow pepper (capsicum)
- 350 g (12 ounces) baby onions
- 20 cherry tomatoes
- 2 fresh Italian pork sausages
- 20 leaves fresh sage
- Sea salt & black pepper
- 2 tablespoons olive oil
- 120 ml (½ cup) beef stock

Special Tip:

These skewers look very attractive so this is a great dish for entertaining friends and family. On special occasions, and once your weight and blood sugar levels are under control, add a few cubes of sourdough bread to the skewers.

Method:

375 CALORIES

Preheat the oven to 200°C (400°F/gas 6). Remove any fat from the meat. Chop the meat and vegetables into large cubes or squares. Slice the sausages thickly.

Thread the cubes of meat and vegetables onto steel or wooden skewers, alternating pieces of meat, sausage, vegetables and sage leaves.

Arrange the skewers in a roasting dish and season with salt and pepper. Drizzle with the oil. Bake for 30 minutes, turning occasionally and basting with the stock to moisten as required.

When the meat is well browned, remove from the oven, and serve hot.

GRILLED STEAK & VEGETABLES

SERVES: 4

Ingredients

4 beef tenderloin steaks, weighing about 150 g (5 ounces) each
3 teaspoons black pepper
Sea salt flakes
4 romaine (cos) lettuce hearts, halved lengthwise
4 medium tomatoes, halved
2 onions, sliced
3 tablespoons olive oil
2 tablespoons butter, melted
120 ml (½ cup) low-fat Caesar salad dressing

Special Tip:

Be sure to choose a light or low-fat Caesar salad dressing for this dish otherwise your calorie count will be much higher.

Method:

430 CALORIES

Rub the steaks with 2 teaspoons of pepper. Season with salt. Chill for 30 minutes.

Prepare a medium-hot fire in an outdoor grill or preheat an indoor grill to medium-high heat. If your grill does not have a solid cook surface, place a grill plate, grill mat or griddle on the grill to preheat. Lightly grease with oil.

Brush the lettuce, tomatoes and onion with oil. Season with salt and pepper. Grill the tomatoes until tender, for 3–4 minutes. Grill the onions until tender, 3–4 minutes. Grill the romaine until heated through, 30 seconds on each side. Push the vegetables to the side of the grill.

Grill the steaks until done to your liking, 5–6 minutes on each side for medium-rare, basting occasionally with butter.

Serve hot, with the vegetables and dressing.

FILLET STEAK WITH MUSHROOMS

SERVES: 4

Ingredients

2 tablespoons olive oil
8 ounces (250 g) mushrooms, thinly sliced
4 spring onions (scallions), thinly sliced
2 cloves garlic, finely chopped
⅔ cup (150 ml) light (single) cream
3 tablespoons fresh lemon juice
1 tablespoon fresh thyme leaves
Sea salt
4 beef fillet steaks, weighing about 180 g (6 ounces) each

Special Tip:

Tender and buttery fillet steaks are packed with protein – about 28 g in each steak.

Method:

400 CALORIES

Heat 1 tablespoon of oil in a large frying pan over medium heat. Add the mushrooms, spring onions and garlic and sauté until softened, about 5 minutes.

Stir in the cream, lemon juice, thyme and salt. Bring to a boil. Simmer over low heat until thickened, about 1 minute.

Heat the remaining tablespoon of oil in a large frying pan over high heat. Add the steaks and cook until done to your liking, 5–7 minutes for medium-rare.

Serve hot with the vegetables.

SLICED STEAK WITH SALAD

SERVES: 4

Ingredients

600 g (1¼ pounds) beef fillet, T-bone, sirloin or rib-eye steak, boned weight
1 tablespoon olive oil
Sea salt & black pepper
2 tablespoons boiling water
120 ml (½ cup) pesto
250 g (5 cups) rocket (arugula) leaves
20 cherry tomatoes, halved
30 g (¼ cup) Parmesan cheese, in shavings

Special Tip: *Steak is rich in protein, vitamins B6 and B12, and magnesium. Trim off any pieces of visible white fat to keep it as lean as possible.*

Method:

500 CALORIES

Preheat a large grill pan (griddle) over medium-high heat.

Lightly oil the steaks and season with salt and pepper. Place on the grill and cook until done to your liking, 4–5 minutes on each side for medium rare.

Remove from the heat and place on a wooden chopping board. Cover with aluminium foil and let rest while you prepare the salad.

Stir the boiling water into the pesto to make it quite liquid. Combine the rocket and tomatoes in a bowl and pour in half the pesto mixture. Season with salt and pepper, tossing well.

Divide the salad among four serving plates. Remove the foil from the steak and slice it about 1 cm (½ inch) thick. Divide evenly among the serving plates. Top with the Parmesan and remaining pesto mixture, and serve hot.

LAMB STEW WITH PEAS & ROSEMARY

SERVES: 4

Ingredients

- 1 tablespoon olive oil
- 1 onion, finely chopped
- 2 stalks celery, sliced
- 2 carrots, sliced
- 2 cloves garlic, finely chopped
- 1 tablespoon chopped fresh rosemary
- 500 g (1 pound) stewing lamb, cut into small cubes
- Sea salt & black pepper
- 120 ml (½ cup) dry white wine
- 3 tomatoes, peeled and chopped
- 300 g (2 cups) frozen peas

Special Tip: *This hearty stew is perfect for cold winter evenings. It has quite a high calorie count so best to serve it at the end of a "light" day.*

Method:

480 CALORIES

Heat the oil in a heavy-bottomed pan over medium heat. Add the onion, celery, carrot, garlic and rosemary and sauté until the vegetables have softened, 7–8 minutes.

Add the lamb, season with salt and pepper, and sauté until browned all over, 5–10 minutes. Pour in the wine and cook until it has evaporated.

Stir in the tomatoes, lower the heat, and partially cover the pan. Cook until the lamb is almost tender, about 1 hour, stirring from time to time.

Add the peas and simmer for 30 minutes more. Serve hot.

LAMB CHOPS WITH CRUSHED PEA MASH

SERVES: 4

Ingredients

- 2 tablespoons olive oil
- 2 tablespoons white wine vinegar
- 2 tablespoons finely chopped fresh mint
- 12 small lamb chops, weighing about 120 g (4 ounces) each, with bone
- Sea salt & black pepper
- 450 g (3 cups) frozen peas
- 2 tablespoons sour cream
- 2 tablespoons freshly grated Parmesan cheese
- Steamed baby carrots, to serve

Special Tip:

Lamb has quite a lot of fat in the meat. Always trim off as much of the visible white fat as possible before you begin cooking it.

Method:

480 CALORIES

Mix the oil, vinegar and mint in a small bowl. Add the lamb and coat well. Season with salt and pepper.

Prepare a hot fire in an outdoor grill or preheat an indoor grill to high heat.

Grill the lamb until cooked to your liking, 4–5 minutes on each side for medium-rare.

Cook the peas in a little lightly salted water until tender, about 5 minutes. Drain and mash with a fork. Stir in the sour cream and Parmesan. Season with salt and pepper.

Serve the lamb hot with the pea purée and carrots.

DESSERTS

Desserts are a great way to celebrate a special occasion but unless your blood sugar levels are perfect and you're not carrying any extra weight, they should really only be served from time to time. In this chapter you will find six simple ideas for low calorie treats that won't do too much damage to your diet. Enjoy!

FRESH FRUIT ICE POPS

SERVES: 8

Ingredients

2 medium white peaches, peeled, pitted & cut into small cubes
2 kiwifruit, peeled & cut into small cubes
150 g (1 cup) blueberries
150 g (1 cup) strawberries, sliced
500 ml (2 cups) pure white grape juice (unsweetened)

Special Tip:

The fruits in these ice pops all have a fairly low glycaemic index and grape juice contains phytonutrients that are believed to help regulate blood sugar levels. Even so, you should not eat more than one of these delicious treats a day.

Method:

88 CALORIES

Combine the peaches, kiwifruit, blueberries and strawberries in a bowl, stirring well to mix.

Divide evenly among eight 3-ounce (90-ml) ice-pop moulds. Press the fruit gently into the moulds.

Pour enough grape juice into each mould to fill all the gaps, making sure that no pockets of air remain. Insert the ice-pop sticks and freeze until solid, at least 6 hours.

BLACKBERRY FROZEN YOGHURT

SERVES: 6

Ingredients

600 g (4 cups) fresh blackberries
2 tablespoons water
180 ml (¾ cup) plain Greek yoghurt
¼ teaspoon stevia
1 tablespoon chopped fresh mint
Nonstick cooking spray
40 g (¼ cup) slivered almonds
¼ teaspoon ground cinnamon
¼ teaspoon ground ginger

Special Tip:

Blackberries have a low glycaemic index. They are also low in calories but rich in dietary fibre. They are an excellent source of vitamin C and other antioxidants.

Method:

130 CALORIES

Combine the blackberries and water in a saucepan over medium heat. Bring to a boil, then reduce the heat to low. Cover and simmer until the berries are softened, stirring occasionally, 4–5 minutes. Remove from the heat and set aside to cool slightly.

Chop the blackberry mixture in a food processor until smooth. Press the puréed berries through a fine-mesh sieve into a bowl.

Whisk the berry purée, yoghurt, stevia and mint in a bowl until well mixed. Cover and chill for at least 4 hours.

Freeze the yogurt mixture in an ice cream machine according to the manufacturer's instructions. Spoon into a freezer-proof container; cover and freeze for 2–4 hours before serving.

Coat a small frying pan with cooking spray. Add the almonds and lightly coat with cooking spray. Dust with the cinnamon and ginger. Toss over medium heat until toasted, 3–4 minutes. Set aside to cool completely.

Scoop the frozen yogurt into six serving bowls. Sprinkle with the almonds, and serve.

ALMOND ICE CREAM

SERVES: 6

Ingredients

500 ml (2 cups) plain Greek yoghurt
250 ml (1 cup) unsweetened almond milk, well chilled
½ teaspoon stevia
1 tablespoon canola oil
½ teaspoon almond essence (extract)
30 g (¼ cup) coarsely chopped almonds
1 tablespoon slivered almonds, to serve

Special Tip:

Serve a scoop of this scrumptious ice cream on hot summer days.

Method:

115 CALORIES

Whisk the yoghurt, almond milk, stevia, oil and almond essence in a bowl until well blended.

Pour the mixture into an ice cream machine and churn according to the manufacturer's instructions. Add the coarsely chopped almonds 1–2 minutes before the machine finishes churning.

Spoon the ice cream into a freezer-proof container, cover and freeze until firm, at least 1 hour.

Scoop the ice cream into serving glasses or bowls, sprinkle with the slivered almonds, and serve.

LEMON TOFU CREAM

SERVES: 4

Ingredients

1 tablespoon finely grated unwaxed lemon zest
¼ cup (60 ml) freshly squeezed lemon juice
1 teaspoon stevia
350 g (12 ounces) silken tofu, firm or extra-firm, drained
150 g (1 cup) fresh raspberries

Special Tip:

Tofu was first made thousands of years ago in China and it is popular in many East and Southeast Asian cuisines.

Method:

75 CALORIES

Combine the lemon zest, lemon juice, honey and tofu in a blender and purée until smooth.

Divide the silky lemon cream evenly among four bowls or serving glasses. Garnish each portion with a sprinkling of raspberries.

Keep chilled until ready to serve.

CHOCOLATE AVOCADO PUDDINGS

SERVES: 4

Ingredients

2 avocados, peeled, pitted & chopped
50 g (⅓ cup) unsweetened or raw cocoa powder
2 tablespoons agave
1 teaspoon pure vanilla essence (extract)
Sea salt flakes, to serve

Special Tip:

These creamy chocolate desserts make a superb treat. If liked, sprinkle with a few fresh blueberries or raspberries or slivered almonds just before serving.

200 CALORIES

Method:

Combine the avocados, cocoa, agave and vanilla in a food processor and chop until smooth.

Spoon the chocolate mixture into serving bowls. Sprinkle lightly with sea salt flakes, and serve.

CHOCOLATE ALMOND ICE CREAM

SERVES: 8

Ingredients

- 1 litre (4 cups) unsweetened almond milk
- 120 g (½ cup) erythritol
- 120 g (1¼ cups) unsweetened or raw cocoa powder
- 1 tablespoon arrowroot
- 1 teaspoon vanilla essence (extract)
- ¼ teaspoon sea salt flakes
- 90 g (½ cup) sugar-free dark chocolate (70%) chips

Special Tip:

Erythritol is a sugar alcohol that occurs naturally in some fruit and fermented foods. It looks and tastes like sugar but has almost no calories and a GI of 1.

Method:

125 CALORIES

Combine the almond milk, erythritol, cocoa, arrowroot, vanilla and salt in blender or food processor and pulse until well mixed.

Pour the mixture into an ice cream machine and churn according to the manufacturer's instructions. Add the chocolate chips to the ice cream when it starts to thicken.

Place in a freezer-proof container and freeze overnight.

Let soften a little by keeping in the refrigerator for 30 minutes before scooping into bowls.